Rescues in Focus

Combat Rescues

by Mark L. Lewis

FOCUS READERS

BEACON

www.focusreaders.com

Focus Readers is distributed by North Star Editions:
sales@northstareditions.com | 888-417-0195

Produced for Focus Readers by Red Line Editorial.

Photographs ©: Alex Lerner/Shutterstock Images, cover, 1; US Department of Defense, 4, 10, 15, 17, 23, 24, 29; US Navy, 6; Carolyn Kaster/AP Images, 9; Tech. Sgt. Christopher Hubenthal/US Air Force, 12; Life Magazine/AP Images, 18–19; Sam Smith/Alamy, 20; Getmilitaryphotos/Shutterstock Images, 27 (left soldier); Philip Pilosian/Shutterstock Images, 27 (helicopter); Tom Weber/Stocktrek Images, Inc./Alamy, 27 (right soldier)

Library of Congress Cataloging-in-Publication Data
Names: Lewis, Mark L., 1991- author.
Title: Combat rescues / by Mark L. Lewis.
Description: Lake Elmo, MN : Focus Readers, [2020] | Series: Rescues in focus |
   Audience: Grade 4 to 6. | Includes bibliographical references and index. |
Identifiers: LCCN 2018056299 (print) | LCCN 2019001269 (ebook) | ISBN
   9781641859783 (PDF) | ISBN 9781641859097 (ebook) | ISBN 9781641857710
   (hardcover) | ISBN 9781641858403 (pbk.)
Subjects: LCSH: Search and rescue operations--Juvenile literature. | Special
   forces (Military science)--Juvenile literature. | Soldiers--Training
   of--Juvenile literature.
Classification: LCC U167.5.S32 (ebook) | LCC U167.5.S32 L49 2020 (print) |
   DDC 356/.16--dc23
LC record available at https://lccn.loc.gov/2018056299

Printed in the United States of America
Mankato, MN
May, 2019

About the Author

Mark L. Lewis lives in Minnesota but has traveled all over the world. He loves writing books for young readers.

Table of Contents

Chapter 1

Rescue in the Desert

A team of US Navy **SEALs** was in Afghanistan in December 2012. The SEALs crossed the desert on foot. They planned to rescue a **hostage**. Enemy fighters had captured Dr. Dilip Joseph.

 Combat rescues often happen in the early hours of the morning when most people are asleep.

 A Navy SEAL's uniform includes many tools that help soldiers do their job.

Four hours later, the SEAL team reached the enemy hideout. A soldier guarded the door.

One SEAL, Nicolas Checque, shot at the guard. Then Checque ran inside. Bullets hit him as he ran. Checque fell to the ground. He was injured.

Team member Edward Byers entered the building next. Inside, he found Dr. Joseph. The hostage was unhurt. Next, the SEAL team cleared the area of enemies. Then they took Dr. Joseph to the helicopter outside.

Byers tried to save Checque. He performed **CPR** in the helicopter.

However, it was too late. Checque died by the time they reached a hospital. He had given his life to rescue the hostage.

Thanks to the SEALs, Dr. Joseph made it home. In 2016, Byers received the Medal of Honor. This medal is the highest award in the US military.

Did You Know?

The mission to save Dr. Joseph lasted only two minutes.

 President Barack Obama awards the Medal of Honor to Edward Byers in 2016.

Chapter 2

Hard Work

Special forces units handle most combat rescues. These military units are trained for difficult missions. For instance, the unit may have to enter a dangerous area. Enemies might be close by.

 The US Navy practices a rescue mission in the Atlantic Ocean.

 Training can push a soldier's body to its limit.

Or a mission may call for unusual **tactics**. For these reasons, only the best soldiers make it into special forces units.

Soldiers work hard to join special forces units. Many spend time in the **infantry**. Others serve as sailors. They build important skills. For example, they learn how to treat injuries. They learn how to escape capture. They also build their body's strength and abilities.

Did You Know?

Spain's special forces unit accepts less than 30 percent of the people who try out.

Special forces soldiers go through difficult training. They must pass challenging tests. For instance, the US Air Force trains combat rescue officers. These officers take a swimming test. They must swim the length of a pool without coming up for air.

Pakistan has one of the best special forces units. These soldiers must be able to march 36 miles (58 km) in one day. They do all this while carrying heavy gear.

> **During a jump, soldiers reach speeds as fast as 120 miles per hour (193 km/h).**

Soldiers train for many types of missions. For example, they learn how to dive. This skill is important for underwater rescues. They also learn how to jump out of airplanes.

This skill helps them enter hard-to-reach places. Soldiers learn **hand-to-hand combat**, too.

In some countries, special forces units have age limits. In France, **recruits** must be under 32 years old. In Russia, they must be between 22 and 27. Many countries require several years of military experience.

Very few soldiers actually finish special forces training. To do so, soldiers must be strong and smart.

 Some soldiers help their unit by looking out for danger.

Also, they must be able to work well with others. These traits help them be the best at their jobs.

The Great Raid

During World War II (1939–1945), Japan captured many **Allied** soldiers. Some of these prisoners lived in camps in the Philippines. One camp held more than 500 people. Japanese leaders ordered the prisoners to be killed. So the United States tried to save them.

US special forces soldiers acted at night. They crawled across a field to the camp. They didn't want the Japanese guards to see them. As planned, a US plane flew overhead. The plane distracted the guards. Then, Filipino fighters helped the US soldiers surprise the guards. They were able to save all the prisoners.

These soldiers were rescued during the Great Raid.

Chapter 3

Saving Lives

Government leaders call special forces only in certain cases. One example is hostage situations. Captors usually want something from the government. They take hostages to get what they want.

 Soldiers often use helicopters to fly rescued soldiers to safety.

The government could try making a deal with the captors. But sometimes, a deal is not possible. In these cases, special forces go in to rescue the hostages.

Combat rescuers must act fast. If captors know a team is coming, they might hurt the hostages.

Did You Know?

SEAL Team Six is a special forces unit in the United States. In 2009, this team rescued a sailor after pirates captured his boat.

 Soldiers practice how to break into a building to rescue hostages.

Instead, rescuers try to surprise the enemy. That way, captors won't be ready to attack.

 Gas masks protect soldiers from unsafe air.

Rescue teams often travel part of the way by helicopter. But helicopters are loud. For this reason, teams finish their journey on foot.

Rescue teams have many types of gear. For example, they may use night-vision goggles. These goggles help soldiers see in the dark. Soldiers also need good boots. They might walk across deserts, streams, or city streets. Their gear needs to be sturdy.

Did You Know?

In 2010, the US military began using a new type of night-vision goggles. They let soldiers see much easier at night.

Combat rescuers need other protection, too. They wear helmets. They wear bulletproof vests. Without this gear, soldiers could be killed. And soldiers always carry weapons to defend themselves.

Each soldier usually carries several weapons. He or she may carry a rifle. The soldier may carry a pistol, too. This small gun goes in a holster attached to the leg. The soldier also carries knives. These can be used as weapons or tools.

helmet

helicopter

gun

night-vision goggles

bulletproof vest

boots

Even with the right tools, soldiers still get hurt. But that is part of the job. Rescue teams risk their lives to save others.

FOCUS ON
Combat Rescues

Write your answers on a separate piece of paper.

1. Write a sentence describing the main idea of Chapter 2.

2. Would you want to join a special forces unit? Why or why not?

3. In which country did the Great Raid take place?
   A. the United States
   B. Japan
   C. the Philippines

4. Why do rescue teams often try to reach hostages on foot?
   A. Walking is faster.
   B. Walking is quieter.
   C. Walking is easier.

5. What does **captors** mean in this book?

Captors usually want something from the government. They take hostages to get what they want.

    A. people who rescue hostages
    B. people who are being held hostage
    C. people who hold others hostage

6. What does **sturdy** mean in this book?

*Soldiers also need good boots. They might walk across deserts, streams, or city streets. Their gear needs to be **sturdy**.*

    A. strong
    B. clean
    C. simple

Answer key on page 32.

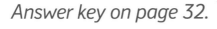

Glossary

Allied
Having to do with the victorious countries of World War II, including the Soviet Union, the United Kingdom, France, and the United States.

CPR
A way of saving someone whose heartbeat or breathing has stopped.

hand-to-hand combat
Fighting that involves physical contact between people at close range.

hostage
A person taken by an enemy force.

infantry
A military force with troops who serve on foot.

recruits
New members of a group.

SEALs
Highly trained soldiers who carry out special operations.

tactics
Planned actions that are used to achieve a certain goal.

To Learn More

BOOKS

Dittmer, Lori. *Helicopters*. Mankato, MN: Creative Education, 2019.

Kiland, Taylor Baldwin. *Military Rifles: Combat Ready*. New York: Enslow Publishing, 2015.

Webb, Brandon. *Navy SEALs: Mission at the Caves*. New York: Henry Holt, 2018.

NOTE TO EDUCATORS

Visit **www.focusreaders.com** to find lesson plans, activities, links, and other resources related to this title.

Index

B
bulletproof vests, 26–27
Byers, Edward, 7–8

C
captors, 21–23
CPR, 7

H
helicopter, 7, 24, 27
helmets, 26–27
hostage, 5, 7–8, 21–22

I
infantry, 13

M
Medal of Honor, 8
military, 8, 11, 16
mission, 8, 11–12, 15

N
night-vision goggles, 25, 27

R
rifle, 26

S
SEALs, 5–8, 22
special forces, 11–14, 16, 18, 21–22

T
tactics, 12

U
underwater rescues, 15
US Air Force, 14
US Navy, 5

W
World War II, 18

Answer Key: 1. Answers will vary; **2.** Answers will vary; **3.** C; **4.** B; **5.** C; **6.** A